Ride Ferris Wheel.

Chapter 1 : The start

12th April 2014
Location : Unknown

He was in his late 20s distorted but focused on learning new things all the time. He thinks struggle leads to new ideas, was reading Godel, Escher and Bach don't know why but this is a journey to understand math from a different perspective where evaluating formal spaces through negative spaces which are not part of positive areas belonging to a sound system.

He was never consistent suggestions put through his own creators and is incomplete just the way our language is. He claimed himself a beginner, follows a path from where returning from such-ness or is thusness, is-ness, emptiness are whole.

According to his theory, time is moving forward, and it is the absolute proof of work and time is the adiabatic process in between obtaining freedom without being aware of the rules mean nothing.

He never understood what Gplot infinitely many infinities means? Recursion happening at a subtle level of the matter was his key take away that day.

It was clear he couldn't reach to the idea which he has in mind, but yes he struggled a lot since then.

He had a memory where his father told him that he could not do anything in life because he was terrible at mathematics.

He is unable to prove himself according to his father's standard, but yet he managed to live a life on its own, in one conversation where one of his friend of his was present his father asked him "What are you doing these days?" He replied, "I am working out a few things and will apply to AIEEE."

Now, AIEEE stands for some exam where you have to compete against millions of other student and have to stand out at least in thousands to score a right college

His father replied, "How do you plan to do that", while eating satvik food.

Wait, but what is satvik food? Well in his world of interpretations he thinks the food which belongs to people who care about the health, or maybe the ones they serve in Hospitals, but food in Hospitals is also much better then satvik food.

Actually, why is he calling this food "Satvik" is quite strange because this food is much below then the standards of satvik ones, maybe it's just that his liking of food is different, so he is afraid to digest this food down his throat.

His brother was eating this same food, and he did not have this problem neither he was referring to this food as "satvik".

So, the one who was preparing this food was his mother. Naturally, he was not aware of the position of her mother in her life, which will haunt him later and shape his life as it is.

"He said, well i am now living life next to DCE and will get a seat there, he claimed," Suddenly his father scattered food on the table and said, " Well, you know you 'don't know and cannot do anything because you are not good at maths." He was bewildered and replied, "You know 'don't try to tell me."

He was not interested in listening to anything because in his life, something else written, the so-called destiny which he was not aware of where spending sleepless night to become what he would never imagine.

He left the room, without saying much and everything was in silence and moved into a different time dimension.

17th Feb 2015
Location: Unknown

More is always different, and I was amazed to see how the world works; it is quite versatile, mind-boggling yet straightforward. I thought let us take a reductionist approach where one can divide everything into the irreducible primary.

Then i realized i would never be able to understand our cognition is coming from where. I am aggregating myself through actions, limiting centrally through a game of life, and playing by preferences.

So I thought let's predict points and understand data, but where is data? Data and patterns tightly hold outcomes were quite elaborate. Adding independent random variables with finite variance would lead me to the normal distribution in life. Oh good lord, i thought that day i am the designer of my life.

Calculations triggered, my neurons so hard that i do not need anyone to teach me anything process has started i was returning.

I am thinking about making some intelligence tool and going to Silicon Valley.

12th Apr 2014
Location : Unknown

Let the thought come and acknowledge them but do not engage in them. Suddenly the idea was killed, and i was involved, why people are not interested in going directly to the news website and reading everything, data overflow.

Ramayan and Mahabharata used extensive commentary as well annotations, non-linear discourses ancient examples of Hypertext. Need to finish my research paper sometime soon about contextual data search.=

Then someday you are an innovator, quest for continuous learning be willing to make mistakes. What makes me wonder this FF =F or ~F > ~(F OR F)=T> T=T.

George Boole invented the above statement, De Morgan gave the duality but wait binary was already dual.

He exploded.

11 Mar 2017
Location: Delhi

I am trying hard to quit certain habits including

Smoking,

I think my day starts with a lot of thoughts which were previously hashed and is now on the increment for the other day.

I am relatively hard to understand why is this happening, but 'it's happening and sometimes i and good at letting things go.

I have to let go of all the fear.

It is that chilling which comes to me when i listen to people i have to let it out.

It's not easy i have tried a lot of times.

I am going to do it.

Today only.

Math is the only answer to my whole issues.

Chapter 2 It all started

1 May 2018
Location : Unknown

I lied to her again that I meeting that psycho therapist…and I am not interested at all….Some lies are good …I think, but I need to be very alert that it should not become anything more than that.

No date
Location: Unknown

I am not the answer and can never be I don't need to find any answers because they are there and there is no need to find anything. Drop the search you are looking for there is no fun in that just be.

When I am going to be, the I is going to get destroyed or the self-conflict will resolve. Self is always in conflict and is looking for an escape.

Ego is a bigger illusion than anything else, and everything I do is not my doing its happening within because of cause and effect.

This time I am going to be no-one. Let it all be. Open eyes and see yourself as you are. The physical universe is your witness.

Go beyond. Take a jump and drown yourself in the truth. The truth of your self which does not exist but lives within you.

This pain is beyond anything.

All of the suffering which I have surmounted on me and is roaming around. I see the world differently.

Ringing through and yet it's not bounded or is it so?

I am just not okay. I think I should not do what I do. Let it be and let things like this.

All of the things I have created in my head and I don't belong here and there and really do not know what to do.

Lying all the time to myself and does not want to understand anything which I want or wish to have.

Desires are purely not mine, and they can never be. All of the rationality once occurred and will occur is not mine, and I am not like this how I portray myself.

My feelings are not all-right they are temporary and yet I am so moved by them.

Let's go into the surface a little bit more.

I want to get intoxicated and run for my desires, which is sex? Look at the patterns, you will get to know everything I want to get physical with different women and just look for some short talks. Just to get through all of this, I am ignoring everything and wearing a mask which I shouldn't do.

I am doing even I am right now in the morning I will wake up with the same thoughts lets try to change some patters tomorrow lets try to be compassionate and do nothing, but wait I am stuck like others hahaha, I have to finish things or else I will not be able to pay my bills….How ironical is this?

Am I alright, I should ask myself.

Get out of the intoxication as soon as possible, right now.

Date unknown
Location: Unknown

I met her, again after long she was happy, but her voice was little changed perhaps, the reason behind her new voice was viral. I left her when she was suffering from viral. I don't know what happens to me whenever I am near to her, close and then on the other side I am doing precisely the opposite.

I am not sure, why am I judging her based on the age, imaging in next life or this life it can happen to me. I mean, I am ready does not mean I can commit a crime and then face punishment. I should not and repent this asap.

So what I am going to do is go to her house and give her this painting where I am going to write all sort of lovely things, and I am going to make her realize that she is beautiful and she can get anything not run away from her.

About priority I think I am in a dilemma with her, I am going prioritize myself, self-obsession is in the new thing. I will always think about me in the first instance. Not about others and waste my time on some other things.

Keep yourself away from all form of drugs in life focus and pay attention to details and act as an observer as if without any judgment and enjoy life to the celebration without anything on a mind. Remove your account away, don't think, move fully wholehearted inside, and everything will come back to you. Drop the ego.

What is ego?

Whatever is essential and related to I. What is I. The form I have attained right now which is null and impermanent

Let that go from me asap.

Date Unknown
Location: Pune

She called me, as usual, my phone was on silent. So I got excited and called her back ...tried several times, was not expecting that she will be back in my thought was trying to tell me something else, but I did not care since I meditated and tried to calm myself by not intoxicating her. Decided not to be distracted from anyone.....left smoking and drinking forever ...I am happy that I am doing something for myself ...like writing down this thought for myself and sharing it with myself.

I was drowning in her thoughts since the morning I don't want to lie to myself anymore about me or others as long as I am sane and sober, today is full moon I remember I used to share this energy with Layla, we used to meditate and walk in the lanes and be present about our feelings.

I never wrote down my feelings so consistently, listening to Sigur Ros. I am liking the fact that I can accept the change which is happening around me without arousing and making any effort when there are some friction and conflict I make, and I don't change.

I am giving pain to myself for things I did not do....I visited Layla also today, but she wanted me to tell her the truth that I love her and left her by saying that I was leaving for smoke and went outside ...but, in reality, I was preparing myself for something else...maybe not even for Simran ...I am preparing myself for something else.......I am not sure confusion is so good because it lets out some kind of clarity, that is what I have realized.

Being in love with yourself is the best thing you can ever have....Breeze just went by felt so cool..........about it.....Just pass by, the clouds are gone even though you 'don't know what is going to happen tomorrow just be and laugh on all the things you can ever have and stop hating yourself...you are no more and will never be same and be yourself as much as possible...

Maybe tomorrow never comes, just be yourself and live this day '...do not think logically too much you have live one-fourth of your life in learning logics now try to drop it. Drop all the nonsense and ego. Just be truthful and act upon things out of compassion, not with ego it will wither away all the love and joy you can ever have life is about celebration not for sadness, although if it comes and accept it as much as possible and be.

'Don't think a thing what is going to happen and what is happening right now...just be and 'don't try to act smart about anything let the head evaporate....

We spent time on the streets by bursting balloons...for me, balloons were like my thought, which were evaporating so fast, and I could see my impermanence and imperfection.

24th Sep 2018
Location Pune

She has written a book about her feelings may be connected to me or not. I am not sure. But I have gone down the drain with her emotions, don't need her validation nor acceptance. I see how people want to express their feelings and make people feel that yearning is still there. They said I listened, ego arises and defines all the walls and turns into a stone. The one which is not there comes into pictures and plays around but this time no running around for anyone. No games just pure heart and nothing else If someone is saying something accept it and move on and don't see it back and if they wish to face you again smile on them like buddha did. Just be, pure not a mixed state of anything.

Let go of the past, It will have no meaning for you and not for everyone, others are trying hard to hold onto the past, will call you names and will try to put in the zone they are, but you have to learn that this body and mind are one.

I am beyond this, so just take a breath and let go of it.

I miss her again, and I wish to be with her not with these assholes. But back then I will never learn anything its just a matter of time.

You have to maintain this energy in you which you have right now. Get rid of toxic waste asap, leave the ego behind, and just be okay.

Why do I even listen to them when I don't like what they say. I am unable to make a decision, that is all because for me I am confused about what is right and wrong, I think I should not ignore and let talk that is all……It will be interesting to see what kind of conversations they will come up and don't answer things just like that.

Sleeping after some meditation met two drunk friends of Simran, said to me that I have sexual tension between her….linger on. Since they did not realize they will put out what they are and going through.

Alone and empty after a long time, both body and mind cannot describe this state…

Not the same state anymore, I am in…I don't want to be. I am out of it.

25th Sep 2018
Location Pune

I was talking to Juhi suddenly, the women I left a long time because I did not and could not be with her perhaps, I have left all the women behind because of this same reason the noise around me. I left people because others were saying something to me about what they could not tell people directly themselves what a shit I am? Really.

I mean I was never in love with anyone except with myself, or probably I have never loved myself, so don't know. The good thing is I have started loving myself, What kind of change is this few years ago I was running away from a similar type of people and looking for something in myself, and now I am talking to similar people. I have to understand this very clearly this time I should not be affected by all of this or am I getting to the same route.

I wanted to show them its possible to observe without affecting yourself.

I went to meet her, and I think she knows this, I am also not sure what is going on. This is for sure there is something between me and her I danced, and she kissed me, I really like her. I am always thinking about her all the time. This goes

Dancing on rhythm.
Unknown to each other.
Love is there.

So I set out to watch her and witness her, and I think she is acting a little different every time. If I am doing the same thing, she is also doing the same and repeating it.

I am not sure what is going to happen? Am I overthinking or its just that I cannot take something against me, or am I changing myself for her?

I see her

I feel her
I touch her
Remove i.
It becomes none.
Everything becomes infinite.

She is sitting next to me, and my thoughts are more stable right now, maybe she does not like me, and she is being forced to do this. She has said this that she is using me physically, But my question from her should be what?

Playing with me.

Date Unknown
Location Pune

She was showing me how her Cat responds to her voice and how the Cat would look back to her. I was looking at her, and none of her callings acknowledged in her cat eardrums.

The way she was calling "Kitty" and with different pitches "and said he understand my calling. In reality, Cat was just interested in licking his body, which is what she likes also. She like cleaning, does all the time, my hair, my body and everything which belongs to me she wants to clean. She understands my calling also. Even if she is far, she will know without much effort.

Whenever i am around, she would start putting things back to their places; I am afraid that she might also put me where I belong. Honestly, i would love to be there where she wants me to be.

I like her idea of showing me two fingers when she is cleaning it means 2 min but can extend up to 15 to 30 min. While she is brushing her bed covers, She would ask me to take care of the Cat because the Cat would jump and try to get hold of anything which is moving. This Cat is different, unlike other cats; this Cat will try to take part in everything, be it cleaning or cooking or even when we were making love.

Nevertheless, the Cat does not listen to her calling now and probably someday will listen to her.

I always listen to her; She does not know that i go into her eyes and see that she is trying to tell me, Saransh. I am afraid, i love you like anything, but you are a free bird and will leave, and i will break again.

Again i don't respond to her, and we lose ourselves in something beyond words.

By now, She knows that I make stories; it's just that we both know those stories are essential for growing out of the common denomination.

I am not looking out, for her i am looking inside myself every time. Keeps me moving all the time.
I might not be the person who does not stop her or tell her that don't do this and that, but this is where we differentiate we respect each other choices and acknowledge them that this is what we want.

We move along like how water flows when it will be stale; we will let other things grow, it will be a different story then we will talk and look into each other eyes and will let each other know what we want.

Cats and dog will only understand this because they can differentiate and yet live among us. She is a goddess; I affirm that. Wait did she?

Date Unknown
Location Pune

See, I need to understand myself, how these things have been created in my childhood, by being abused and betrayed by my parents and brother and then having nobody else to rely on for food and shelter later these same people who beat me, revealed, manipulated me. I will have to come back to them and force myself to trust the betrayers and abusers themselves!

It's a foul and harmful thing indeed, because, I had no choice at that time, over and over again!

Created a split in me and a trauma bonding[i].

I have to trust the betrayers and abusers to survive! That's 'cognitive dissonance'[2]

It became a pattern in my brain and mind, so later on, in life, I have always been with people who manipulate, abuse and betray, because I feel and think I deserve it.

It made me think that I deserve that only, by abusing, beating, trashing in private and publicly.

I started believing as a helpless child, that I deserve that only. Because a child is innocent and he has nothing to rely upon and trust except the parents, the family.

Does it make sense to me?

This is how 'cognitive dissonance' and 'split' had formed,
 acting against myself and finding betrayal, again and again,
Choosing the wrong people and wrong situations, because parents, family created a pattern in mind when i was a child, I had no choice but to trust the people who harms the most.

Remember, that this was a survival tactic and it was helpful for some point in time because I had no choice.

It became a pattern and a habit in me, a belief, so that later on in life, though I had much better choices and, I found much better people, I still acted on the childhood belief and unconscious pattern, by always choosing to go back to the manipulators and betrayers and the most harmful people. Deep down feeling, I deserve that only that's why I kept betraying myself again and again at nausea, and not understanding my very own acting based on an outdated belief from childhood which has no reality at all.

does it makes sense, do I recognize this pattern in life, in all of my relationships?

Date Unknown
Location Pune

Simran messaged me how you are?
I could not realize that it was her in disguise.
I was replying without thinking anything.
Whoever she was trying to be, she was acting as she knows me,

I was amazed by the fact that who is she?
I thought it was something of the past. Something of this sort has happened already.
Some German women claiming to be a friend, using words such as love and darling and knew me pretty well
But she was acting strange, never answering my phone call, or wishing to meet me and then saying she has left.
I knew it was someone who is playing with me.
So. Did not pay much attention to it then?

But then yesterday Simran did the same thing talking in the same way, not the same but little different this time
But yeah similar style I would say.
She cooked up a story, and I kept saying no that I cannot do anything like this.
Perhaps she was testing me, but what is this test about, if someone sends me a message with information its likely that I will be falling in the pit because another party, has information about me.

She was using the information on max; It is evident that in my head it was not Kajal because I don't remember giving the number to any Kajal.
She might be thinking, and I am that free, I believe this is not loving.
My whole idea about her that she is lovely and considerate is gone in the air now.
Now I am bound to think so many other things which are brutally killing for me now.
No matter how I hard I try, I will think things which are not right.

This little pervert is. I am doing all of this to me; my ego comes into the picture now. Why am i doing all of this?

If she wants something from me, why can't she ask me? I am all over her now, and she is doing this kind of stupid shit which does not make any sense.
It shows more about her personality. Rather than mine.
Making me realize that I am like this, I was always like this. It showed the dark side, what kind of things this bitch is capable.

I am trying to understand what other possible outcomes could have been; I think all of them will reflect a lot about her.
About me, I think its quite simple.

Ok, another side of this story is :

Maybe she is like this, and she needs time to grow as a mature person where she can understand that distance does not mean that one has to inform about everything to each other one needs to be aware and have some trust within themselves also. It does not say that one is morally hazardous. I also understand that i did something wrong in the past so it could be the reciprocation. After looking at her messages to me after the incident.

She did not plan.

Date Somewhere in September 2018
Location Pune

She has returned everything, Its all gone not coming back, now but that does not mean that I have to be lost and act like that I cannot live without her.

Be yourself and don't destroy yourself.

This is where everything changes. Nothing to destroy, nothing to take anything back. Go deeper inside you, and you will realize that there are many things you can do within yourself.

Heal yourself with people who wish to help you. Understand your needs, understand yourself before you know others.

Now, this chapter has ended on a good note, at-least Forget about your house of cards. Maybe I was in denial, and now I am a little bit awake, you can do this just a little bit more of the push is required.

You know what happened precisely ->

I left my lover to be a lover of someone else, whom I was not even aware of, perhaps this was just an attraction but quite sturdy.

This is how we are, I think it all happened because I wanted to try out how does it feel when you betray someone, I was pushed and tossed around in the sky.

Suffering to its best.

Now I know how one plays the game in the field of love. It's quite monstrous, How we are fucking up ourselves so badly and hurting ourselves from inside.

Date Somewhere in September
Location Pune

I started my day just like a bird looking for something, a worm maybe. I was meeting her couple of times but did not realize that it will go this far.

I think I want to be with her, why am I contradicting all of my self. Again and again. Wondering about my own feelings, I think its gonna take a long time to resolve such things, we are falling apart from each other's hand and then we will realize that it's too late.

When you know all of these things are going to happen, why are you doing this, thinking even about all of these thoughts are not right. I guess just observe and watch what is happening to you again, Nah not yet, this time don't do anything don't make any effort.

When you are trying hard to do something, its spoiled and then you are stuck in a loop which you can never get out. I think you are making it hard for yourself and thus making it hard for your own growth, which seems to be connected with your own past.

Past is magnificent does not end anywhere, its ever-flowing, flowing like a flower which flows inside your head and turns out that it is outside. Do you know what I mean? This is for real.

She is asking me to leave. She will become someone else, which is she is not.
This is true.

What do I have to do with this? I am running after her now. I think I have to also tell her that this process has started and I will rest when things become on its own. Let me not hurry for anything.

Date Around December
Location Pune

The idea of love is quite simple and I, wish to be in it even though my opinions differ from everyone, Do I, really know what love is?

Nevertheless, I will not be answering any of the typical questions which, everyone around me is looking. I will put all of my pure thoughts without putting the idea that it defines me or my beliefs put me into a zone where it leads to creating self-referencing patterns.

My interpretations are my own, but they are meaningful let me put it out.

Carlile book advocates the balance between sex and love[ii]. Carlile mentioned, our social arrangements are very much opposed to physical wants as an animal, and he looks at the nature of this passion as something of more importance than the social arrangement

First, ask what love is?
Relate with your own experience with it.

Elusive nature of love, It may be defined as the growth of unknown origin, which may take up its site anywhere without the subject of knowing or wishing it. How often have you tried to love the right person in vain even when your heart knows it has found him after so much seeking? No, an eyelash, a perfume, a strawberry on the neck, the smell of almonds on the breath - these are the accomplices the spirit seeks to plan your overthrow.

Many tried to explain love but failed in despair.

Interpersonal attraction

Fear arouses romance in human being. Rejection leads to anger, hatred, which can also be labeled as love sometimes.
Frustration and challenges,
Poorly articulated information surrounding us gives us a wrong interpretation of love.

Labeling your emotions as love is what we are doing, all the time. We think if we are aroused and have specific thoughts which we can explain, we will label it as love.

Date End of December 2018
Location Kerala

I was frustrated at that place, Pune with the people around me it was a terrible idea even to exist there, all of them wanting something from my co-existence, I was unaware of what I did, I asked or convinced her that I love her with all of my drama, and she supposedly believed it , that was way too easy.

Hey, wait I do like her then why I am calling it a tragedy, this I what I do, I don't have words with me, which also does mean that I am not reading enough every day.

I am following my full heart, I am acting at the moment, As usual, I was in stress because I didn't ask someone to come with me, and while getting out of her house I stole money from her wallet, knowing that she does not have enough. If that's not what stealing is, then what is these American's doing in African countries tricking people and with a beautiful smile stealing natural resources from them.

I was walking down MG road, with few fellow acquaintances, one of them is supposedly a guy who gives excuses of smoking pot because he is growing/working into hemp, but he is not smoking hemp, what he is smoking his marijuana, which he wants to get high again upon his terrace calling himself originals.

Another one is much crazier she is into music, so she has won the entitlement of smoking pot is to get high and analyze music.

Another one was missing because she had periods and I stole money from her, so she was angry at me, she did not want to join us.

That day was quiet and different.

And finally, about me, It's not hard to describe myself, I am a little bit crazier than the above, I don't find any excuse for doing things which I like, I am doing things full power.

That's how I can best describe them.

Walking down MG road, one pothead asked me where I can get some crazy lemon corn.

We stopped by in a corner where someone was selling Rajasthani shoes and sandals for women, as usual, attracted towards the same energy i witnessed years ago.

There it was, Two women who looked, Asian and European or American. They both were white so foreigner, and then we pretended like we also want shoes.
What we wanted to do is to talk to those two women, and when they were leaving they started looking to me as if It is planned (things were happening in my brain) I said Hello, my name is Saransh and this car is my house would you like to join my endeavor

for finding truth within myself. They ultimately accepted me as who I am, at least for then.

Lucia and Merilisa said i look like some actors they knew, one of them is Antonio and some other actor i don't remember the name.

Sometimes people are stupid, Merilisa wanted to drink lemon juice but not on the roadside and said we could go anywhere you guys are going to get what lemon juice.

"Hey, I love you the way I look at you, whatever you accept my love for you at this moment, which is flowing at thousands of light year or maybe faster than the speed of light."

"I would be reaching to you faster than your thoughts, accept me as your lover and released from this world, the more appropriate word is "Fannah."

Well, these thoughts were mine finally, but I said it on my terms.

Then came this person.

Before going to any restaurant, she wants to meditate inside my house and inside my head oh wow, I am getting a chance to contemplate finally inside my car, since Simran and I were fighting inside that car only, and the energy was disturbed she brought the power down to earth.

Ok, so I am a programmer and yes I deal in bitcoins, closely associated with fundamentals of my life, which everyone calls philosophy with me. I was at that time trying to convert some bitcoins to fiat, but as usual, it was a long process, and I couldn't spend time. With the above beautiful women, they were looking for me and especially the one meditated inside my house, I was interested in her.

I was busy while taking care of my exchange and ordering wine, getting drunk, and meanwhile, Simran was asking me where you are? I was coming and going inside the restaurant checking my phone for the transactions.

I danced a bit, but I couldn't talk, I think I realized that after inviting someone, like this one can feel offended or left out.

Another exciting thing about these women was, they were attending some friends marriage in Pune, and few of the friends visiting the same wedding was also in the same restaurant, but they did not ask these women to come along, god knows why and what was happening in their head.

That day I wanted to talk to her but couldn't do it, so I started sending her or her friend messages to meet me, I desperately wanted to get out of Pune, so It was an active catalyst then and there.

I was looking for her so that I can get some pleasure or meet her with some of my thoughts which I was holding for her.

Then the day arrived, she was there, but for some minutes I would say, she was drinking the same drink which I shared with her as if she did not forget anything of my existence from previous lives and previous days or minutes.

I was happy to see her with charged energy and to see her around me; It was my pleasure.

Then as they say it was a good night and they left, while leaving she asked me do you want to go to a festival in Germany with me, I said why not and expressed myself stating that why not now, I can come with you to Goa, she said not this time.

I wonder what triggered me to get out of Pune, Maybe Simran because she was telling me how can you be so pally with those women in front of my presence and had all that drama.

Then around morning time 5.40, I left Pune broke all the past like threads entangled in on another forgot everything about who i am and what i was, Asif was sleeping in my car, so I decided to include him in my journey towards the meeting of two souls. Not sure what she was thinking or having thought about my existence but I continued

I was wondering what I was doing for a moment; the choice of doing something like this makes me realize that I don't respect others or their emotions where my focused effort are selfish.

I left Pune because I was frustrated with myself because i need to do what i have to connect myself with one-ness and hold and let it go and come back and always remain there all the time. I only have today; Now i am living.

So reaching to Goa was naturally comfortable, drove with max gas. I had fuel, and everything sorted we stopped by multiple places ate at different locations.

I was getting calls from Simran, she was asking me for some help.

I was continually ignoring calls from her; I don't know why, because I wanted to tell her the truth, actually I speak the truth but with some delay.

I was waiting to see her; I don't know why that too, it is like complete riding on edge,

So around evening I sent her a message that I am in Goa, she said come and I will see you believe it, I was excited, got flowers for her from the Gulmohar tree. Everything is so fucking natural and insane; everything was available for me whenever needed without making any effort, and all I have to smile.

I think today it all ended i wanted to express myself, so i went out so far, Am i a psychopath?

Or to say or speak regulate love through me.

I saw her and realized she is different and small, but she felt pleased seeing me, I was a little bit holding myself back, by not going too much, I think it is not good. I need to go to it. I did not hug her i stopped myself.

She was in the hostel, surrounded by her inmates from there, I could see that she was conservative about her self, wanting but was not doing it correctly, shared with me what she did that day, and now tired in the evening.

I was going to ask her to come with me, but it was apparent now i cannot do that.

I told her that i took a bath in a river next to a victorian bridge build in 1854.

Our meeting was like two lost lovers met after a long time and is trying to express themselves.

I was a bit afraid what if they have their plans to travel around Goa, so this is how it will go

1. I was going to wait and make plans and sleep in the car for the next few days.

2. To understand the one i am interested.

She also told me that she is a nun. i was like what the fuck is that?

The last women i was with also told me the same, and before that was telling me that all other women are a nun. I think both of them were right.

I was actually not doing what i need to do, but i am also not sure what to do, i called it a night.

I was doing it, bit by bit,

I don't know what was it about, was it about her. Honestly, it was not about her. I think It is about some Leela which I have in my mind.

Another thing about her she has some calming energy, like water where she is peaceful, her eyes reflect that, but she was nervous today.

I was waiting to be alone with her, where I can talk to her eyes to eyes which happened today.

She was like the river flowing in herself; I liked around her. She invited me to some temple, next to her Ashram where she is staying.

We sat next to a bathing area inside the temple which was like placidity, album art from the music album.

She was nervous, and I was calmly looking at her in her eyes is so delightful, that I wish I could have her eyes, those Stories she has gone through them. I want to be part of it.

I gave her pomegranate diffuser, oil it was excellent. She asked me was it for you or me, I said I had used it, but now you can take it and then there will be some excuse for us to meet if I ever wanted it back.

She laughed.

I laughed.

There was a frog inside the pond; she started throwing rocks and pebbles towards the frog. I was watching her.

But the frog was not giving a fuck.

I asked her will you marry me; she said, do you have a ring.

I looked around and used some natural fiber to make a small circle not a ring; she did not like, I guess, she removed it after some time.

She told me before if stars are aligned, we can marry, and I started looking at the online marriage match calculator, so it turned out that I cannot read anything from those charts it prepared, but it turned out that I am Aquarius.

She looked at me and said, are you Aquarius? I said no idea.

So, she was saying that it's quite surprising for her, that how it happened what is happening right now and she told me that she was supposed to be here at 24th, but then another friend also wanted to come with her, and she met me along the way, she referred to this as confusion (She called me a snake). Cleary i was in between something and took her out from her goal, that is what i do, i am so intense why not use this energy somewhere else.

But then it got late; I can see that she is doing this to peace her out because she cannot do this back in her country (or maybe she can do these things here) mediation and yoga-practicing and what not to let her energy rise higher.

She was saying that do not change your plans for me; I said I would see that. I wanted to change my plans so desperately that I will dissolve all of my ideas for someone else.

I think she is doing all of this because she does not want me to feel bad, I don't understand this but I won't if she says no to me, I would like to move on faster. (Though she said no when i asked her to kiss me). She also mentioned, it is not a vacation and is uncomfortable. I did not like, but i digested it firmly.

Let me see how it works out.

Date July 2019
Location Delhi

I have been thinking that I have to stop living in denial have to be more constructive now and then,

Have to propel I am choosing what i am right now that last I can change.
All I have left is the distant memories of all the ones.

Now, another time is something beautiful.
I feel like moving away from all the worldly things.
Suddenly the urge is quite strong.

I want to live on a bare minimum.
I want to be able to save the resource for this planet.

Yesterday I saw life growing alongside with a new person entering in my family. It was never my family; I was just born there.

Now, I know who can do what and what roles does it play.
I am a little bit disturbed about the fact that everything that I know so far is dissolving,

It's quite visible that there are some worries
There are some questions
There are.
Yes.

Date May 2019
Location Mumbai, Colaba

Have to leave some behind, Oh yeah I had an erection in the night thinking about her again while planning how I could take her out with me and would make love to her.

What: But this time is different since this time I was watching myself so clearly that It came out as something beautiful

Today what happened is the signal that I am on the right path but wrong output it should have been burning, and I am here burning alive.

Date June 2019
Location Delhi

All of them just left, I am here with myself
Going closer, today there is some bubble did it come because I lost money.

So, it's my desires moving across the sea; this is not good.

I am glad I did not let direct my whole thought process and made me do things which I don't want.

Although I enjoyed a massage from the strong hands,
It feels like I am now not doing anything, who am I making this excuse you are doing everything.

What is that you are following, I have to stop somewhere.

I think I am moving too fast but where is the answer, to all of the things what I am of right now.

My parents want to be with them. It seems like things have changed as I wanted them, I need to stop saying things because I am doing something, else I have to let the whole course decide since I am a god I can do, Whatever I feel, like.

Conserve energy as much as possible this time watch more and more what you do.

Move inside just the way you are; Maybe there is a way where you can leave everything and be where by you want to know the answer, and I think I tried it hard.

I have sent all of my ideas out in the world trained people, and how they want, what they wish to do. Job is done for some time, its time to come back and see what is inside.

Just letting things go out, you have to find no way there is no way its a not. A dead-end, whatever you are doing is following it but don't question and tire yourself take some good rest since she is a queen of understanding where you could take rest.

Date 29th March 2019
Location Goa

There is us, and there is him, what was his name "A S Salkar."
I asked him where are you from "He said talk something else doesn't talk about me you can talk about your own story."

I was like hey this is my story and who gives a shit about your account. I am trying to get to know your system your inner working so that I can infect you by my operations, but there seems like a hard wall around this police officer he does not take any input from my functions or system it appears like he is enjoying everything whatever we are trying to tell him.

He thinks we are quite casual and seems like we don't care about our surrounding. I did not reflect at that moment what he was saying because there was no time in my head, you know what my thought was I was super tired and wanted to get out of that place.

Emily opened the door, and she was asking for Paracetamol and Asif went to help her, I heard the conversation from all around, I know something was going on but not sure which story to follow this ignited the passion for writing since the cop did not like my casual attitude.

A customs officer stopped us ☐♂▢ it was election time in India, quite unusual I mean in my entire time traveling in India; I did not see anything like as such a level where you could be stopped and inspected by an on-police officer. Something fishy I mean, who goes on to this extent, who are they trying to control or stop or put limits on.

The government should keep a global ledger of ownership since this was a matter of property of something which police identified as illegal to carry. In the first place, the system is so brokem that information is inadequate.

I was happy that I found a place where I can now pitch my business proposition I was doing for this German company finding a house and creating a research facility. We were in South Goa, the whole day was exciting, and it became spicier as we moved along.

The day before yesterday I had a conversation about us traveling together, I was trying to explain Asif that what is that he is counting on us or vice versa, maybe he should work some other model with us.

As he said, I am your friend, and I expect my friends to do certain things for me, which are obligatory.

I said sure and asked like what, he spoke like spending on food, and added no one asks in return for food. I said, I can understand that totally because I have not been bothered with that, but when it comes to an explanation for Emily it becomes hard for me and then when I try to query Asif it becomes exciting like as if it's his right and there should be no bargain with that.

Emily was sick because she was unhappy about the fact that we were going to leave her; she wanted to be with both of us. Maybe with Asif, when I was in Gokarna fucking her in my wild dreams, but it was my ex GF who I was making love.

Asif was telling me that she was not eating food, since Auroville, because in Auroville the food quality was amazing, cooked by personalities hanging on spiritual.

She was sick; we took her to some hospital, don't remember, the exciting thing I could see or at least define their characters.

Maria was interested in leaving to France, so she was with us. She was not bothered what was happening around.

Asif was interested in saving money and taking her and giving her injections and glucose.

I was interested in making money and going to Europe.

All ended at five o clock.

Date 20th August 2018
Location Pune

I met her where she was with her past.
You are bound to lose her in the first moment.
Then suddenly bumped in her and I asked her to meet me.
Did not realize that she would come closer in a few days.
We went out together.
I was watching her expressions; she was collecting dust in this space.
I invoked her thoughts of something back in the past.

Looked at her again, She asked me I can walk with you, and I said no, I wish to walk alone.

She said okay and hugged me then she left.
I went back and lost interest got involved in my life, which does not seem to exist.

Have gone berserk.
You lost in her thoughts. Quite nice.

Then I should meet her once again and ask her what her plan is?
Lost her again and this started which I was not expecting.
Since I did not know, anything about her.
I was looking for her all day.
She is gone forever.
Let's go back where I was and travel ahead.

Got back and asked her, "Wish to make love with you," her wall melted.
She hesitated, but she was in front of me, and we were holding each other's hand.

Her hands in my hand, her soul within my frame, her energy became mine.
She was scared, asked me, "This is it?" What do you want?
She gave me options. We meet and say hi to each other or do you want to meet me again with some different feelings in your heart.
Realized I am again going to euphoria.
She was not paying attention to whatever I was saying.

She was controlling all of the outcomes so persistently and that she does not want to let go.
We met again and again; she liked being with me. I loved it too.
I could see the trauma in her eyes, body.
I could heal her, but what a fool I cannot fix myself and trying to repair another being.
I tried and tried, and my past came in between, it was pulling me back, but I am bright enough and did not dwell in it.
Maybe I am a fool.

My experiences with her body were beautiful, full of lust.
Sexually charged and I like her body there is no harm and shame in that.

She never allowed me to be with her ultimately, just some bits and pieces all I could collect.
I wanted more from me and her also.
It seems like between us, that point never integrated into a finite line of continuous motion.
She still thinks that I would walk away from another point if she walks with me.
I cannot guarantee it.
I told her what was in my mind and heart.

She did not like it. All of the things were disgusting for her.
Maybe she did not want to be with me.
Or I was forcing her all the time.

She came to me a couple of times; actually, I invited her, she said let's go and meet my friends
Pretty hesitant I was, but then It resolved, I think my truth lies within me, and I project what I am not.
Then one day I touched her, she was crying. I was sad, did I hurt her.
She did not say much, and she was back on her feet.
Hot water boiled on and she took a bath she said lets, go.

We were always meeting late in the nights where we were strolling around the streets.
I am routing back to home usually in the morning.
We started sleeping together, wouldn't say anything about it.
This time I was going through my previous relationship
She loved me like her child.
She provided me love all I could need and learned how to be.
I unconditionally love someone without much ado.

Date 20th October 2019
Location Goa

There was a time where he did not like me.
I never paid attention to him and did not show him any affection.
Cursed him, sent him hatred instead of love.
We had something else going on with each other.
I could feel it he was disappointed with certain things I did.
But I never wanted his attention towards me.

Time goes by he came back and said things which I did not wish to hear.
He is controlling himself a lot, and I could see his fate so determined.
Profoundly he said, Reality is getting distorted. I asked him why don't you relax and let go of everything.
He said, no, I cannot because then I won't feel secure.
I said, take the risk and see what happens.

Break the pattern don't get involved with any your thoughts.

He said, no this is your Reality, and this is mine.
I said you fool, without even trying this and that you are putting me in a cage.
He was continually contradicting himself; his game was simple.
I could feel it he was not here because of me.
It was his need which took him here.

I am like a duck, walking on the shores and looking for food without any conflict
I invited him, did not tell him anything because for him to be.
I need to require an infinite possibility.
Told him only one thing, let go into waters, he was scared.
I could see his bond with nature is not so good as it seems.
I could feel his control going away, every moment he was fading away and was not liking everything which was happening.
At this point, he would say, It's my perception from this point of incidence and angles.

I said to him, What is your status of sexuality? He thought I was asking him to engage in intercourse; he came with the same
The argument, I will do when I feel.
I replied, What are you saying? There was a disconnect, and I could feel he went away from that talk. Something was wrong and mechanical with him.

Rest is the history which I am not interested in.

Date Unknown

Location Unknown

Same things are happening with me like everything is repeating itself.

Everyone is eating biryani, isn't it all grouped.

I as a human
Repeating everything
Not going beyond this karmic circle
Repeating everything
Beyond this I have ideas
Ideas which sprout within me
Causes me to do certain things which are not my doing.
Sunlight
Provides me a stable region to cast my shadow
Destroyed everything which we could create.
We have consumed everything which we could.
I and I became we just as I see.
Not all the sides are turned, but it is still unheard.
You are allowed inside me, but don't turn my face next to you.
I will reflect so hard that you won't be able to return from your reflection.

Its infinite everything, recursions are life.
I am living with people who once never liked me.
Just watch. The play. How the dance happen.

Date Unknown
Location Unknown

All of a sudden it all started and I am in a motion which nobody could halt. I am same, and others are all also same, she asked me how you can be so self - righteous, I said I am not, the fun starts from you.

All of these days were like similar kind of instances. I felt, and I see how my past is coming in front of my eyes as if some competition was there a certain hesitation about others was there.

I am not sure what to do in this kind of instances, and I think the best is to make sure that it does not affect you. Right now, I am getting bombarded with specific situations.

I have invited back those same people who were unhappy with me but could not let me ever know what they are trying to speak.

Slowly some of them said it's over, and some came up with something else which I could not comprehend, I am observing too much, too much going into details, come back to yourself and decide once for all because it's about you and not about something else.

You know, go beyond ideas, every trail of thoughts which you have right now
It seems like.

Date Unknown
Location Pune

Again, with her, someone forced me to think things about her. It's not right she said she is a nun, I am repeating those words like a parrot not concerned about the actions which I am bringing from these things, which I am doing, I don't like all of this, but I am doing it. It was a short-lived moment which happened around me. I think I am not doing fine, or maybe I should stop blaming myself.

I think what I told her is something which is coming from outside and it is not my thought, I guess I should say to her this and be honest about what is happening. Is this thought mine or nothing is yours? It cannot be yours. It can never be yours.

It was never yours, and It is you inside you.

I don't want to think about anything right now. My stomach is massive, and my feelings are not alright, I said to Simran, things which I should not have said, but what can I do I couldn't stop myself, I was playing with her, she was also playing with me. It took a different turn where it should not go, but it did maybe possibly this is the end which it should have happened earlier, I was with her because of her body who am I lying to, but it went somewhere else because I am so natural in this. I am so fucking in it, how could it be possible that it can happen.

I did it now, and I am aware why not run because I wish to explain myself so better it does not leave any remarks on her, I feel like that these temporary feelings will hurt me a lot soon.

I will have to pay these feelings dearly because it's going to cost me a lot in myself. It will be like another dent on my body and mind. My mind and body will not be here. But it will go inside my tea the tea which is going to be always there as demonstrated.

You know what happened today was nothing but just my way of doing things, I think I speak, and I don't think about it, and it does fuck me a lot, and I am again not thinking about certain excellent things. I am just going more inside because of this.

One way of looking at this truthful event is from correspondent theory , that my true beliefs and state of affairs reflects my original thought process and how do I relate to the above thoughts, such as I said, if I was a woman "I am vulnerable, and everyone takes advantage of my own body which I also like getting involved"

What if all of this is also a drama just like other plays I did? I don't wish to be in my head. Why am I even thinking right now? About me and anybody else.

Date Unknown
Location Unknown

All of the while.
I am standing in the middle.
Observing everything I could do.

How do you feel?

I wish to meet her. But this has to pass.
I wish to make love with her. It has to pass.
I wish to hang around with her, but it has to pass.
It has to go eventually.
What remains is you and your self.
Which will also pass and dissolve. Hmm.
I take a deep breath.
My heart pounds.
My life stops.
I die in myself.
I am born again.
Everything seems so.
Yeah like here.

My heart goes again here and there for her.

Why is it happening again and again?
Maybe watch yourself, perhaps you need someone all the time.
No matter how hard I try, I am repeating all of my thoughts, why is that so?

Have I ever tried to be with them without affecting me? No perhaps, this is the time to try all of that.

I guess I had lost my path.
I have to get things back in line.
See you soon.
Need some time.

It will pass also.
I left the traveler there, are you still carrying him.
If you love me so much, come and embrace me now.

An old tree grows on a cold rock in winter.
Nowhere is there any warmth.

I am departing from this world.
You are those waves.
Take away the moon

Is that so?

Date Unknown

Location Unknown

I am full of speculation and opinions, first, empty yourself.
When I know everything is impermanent.
Is that so?

Date September 2018
Location Pune

I am not sure what is going, I am afraid again, I think I am. I am not sure what is the reason, maybe I know what the reason is, I was not working correctly from the last few days. I think it could be because of that, that thing, Aha don't blame it to others now grow up and take full responsibility for your actions.

Don't run from them because they will come after you at some point facing them also if not going to make you reliable, don't react at all, learn to create and find the essence.

My heart is heavy again because I am going through some changes which are good and evil and right and wrong …confusing and bright but still you are here with yourself. Don't try to overanalyze anything you will find your self in some game full of rules, leave it.

Leave everything behind, women, sex, drugs and everything which bothers you so much. Don't change yourself so much for someone else, because the moment you are going to do that. You have lost yourself inside the world; this jail is so small inside a bigger frame of prisons.

Learn to find your own thoughts which are lost inside you or someone else ,leave all the support you can have from anyone else

,take your actions and thoughts away from yourself and find yourself outside and don't try to understand who you are because everything is going to be futile whatever you are going to do.

Stop behaving like as if you are, or have something. Let others analyze you and let others direct their projection but don't change yourself for someone else. Be your hero and everything else. It does not mean you have to put yourself on top, put yourself on your self instead of putting your self, at some other-self. Everybody is trying to be someone else, someone they always wish to be. But they have created this also a game, I have created this also a game which does not seem to end, it will end I know when I know very well when it will end.

I know.
Rest is there.
Don't accumulate anything behind.
Past is futile.
Burn everything and let everything burn you.
Be.
Live and die.
Find yourself.
Oh, I am already there.
What is fun? Then, I asked myself.
It could be simpler if you had never tried.
But still, you want to go around the whole world.

Everything seems to be coming back, with the same intensity ,I am living my childhood , my fear has become my own will , my own will has become me, my sadness does not stop anymore and stagnates me anymore, my machine has no cause and effect its all directed and acted and concentrated towards only single thing.

Be.

Date September 2018
Location Pune

I called her in the midnight; her voice distorted. I said I could come and help you heal. She said you need to be calm and quiet because we cannot have that same energy again. Met her after a long time, all of my past just arrived at the same movement how we were, there it was I knew it its is happening but as I am, letting it go things went by.

I took a shower, in her temple, felt nice though had chest pain. Ignored all the signals body was providing, yet I arrived.

Scene 2 :
I was prepared to tell her everything that how I love her and how things were happening, inside is coming outside. I was getting more aware of my position in this vast existence. We lied down in the same bed, I told her that I wish to be like this a free bird, and shared my versions of thought patterns which were happening these days. I thought we could be good friends where she will be my guide in life and share her good experiences with me, joy, flowers, and love without making any effort.

All of my thoughts were breaking and falling apart; how do glasses fall in a city full of ghost. She started again in the same manner, and I told her that I do not wish to be in some relationship where we get involved and get labeled, though I am not sure, I mean all I wanted to say to her I think we should stop with all of the things which we were doing. I want to be a good friend with you why cannot it happen. Why?

I was always from the last few weeks trying to reach her, because of my guilt perhaps and she was throwing fire at me. I need to heal her at any cost because I did this to her. But as I see, I think I am a fool...who is just not letting go of certain things, I have to explore what is inside me, which is pulling me towards her.

I was trying to tell her that I do not wish to do certain things which I wanted.

She messaged Simran that i was fucking her the other night.

Date Long days no idea when?
Location Pune

Could not write from few days. Was busy doing things for my new friend, thanks to her I have realized so many exciting things.

1. Everything is so temporary that even your thoughts do not stay permanent.

2. I never loved Layla; her love was unconditional to me.

3. Layla gave me a better outlook at life; whatever I am right is because of her.

4. I think there is nothing wrong in going back to Layla and pleading guilty to her, Layla's heart is open. Tell her that how and what you saw?

5. Thus that is how the world, its quite fucked up including Layla was living and making me happy everything was there, and I destroyed it and destroyed everything that could and needed.

6. Only love can heal those scars.

7. Learned how to love someone unconditionally.

8. Intoxication is bad. Fucks your temple and leave you an ashtray

9. Learn how to be in yourself while not letting your thoughts affect you.

10. I am still here; how could these problems seem so big. But I am still here.

Date 10th July 2019
Location Banaras

Wandering through ghats of Benaras (Varanasi) lost in our objective world, searching for a place anywhere we could find good coffee and power source.

We wanted to go to Lucy; the name has a lot to do in my life, Once, Lucy said to me you have a good voice, it was my other half who loved her not me, i made sure we meet, in this world under the full moonlight.

We never met the union was there but not through my body. We moved and then we arrived at Lucy.

I was asked to sit outside lucy, Anurag said let's sit upstairs, I answered let's sit outside for a while not knowing how she would enter into my life from the same door i wish to wait for her.

She looked outside, and i was playing flute outside the door, the silence was there it was her who would shape me for the incoming stillness, my full moon.

When i looked at her, it was mostly a girl of the 21st century; her face was outwards, smiling at me as if she knew me, slender in shape, short haircut and was wearing pop culture converse sneaker. (Typically dressed in jeans (21st century)). There was a meaning attached to her outwardly looks, but i dropped it for the sake of my understanding.

When she came closer at that moment my body(in my belly) gripped in some response by her calls, it was invisible. Some explosions of a different kind it was anxiety i suppose.

I get excited when i meet them who is usually practicing some form of isolation through inner work. Priya was different, but sooner i realized her mode of communication is different just like sometimes i communicate through my eyes or my leg or my feelings.

I could feel she was reserved, I asked her something, and she wrote down on note pad   "I am sorry, i have taken silence to get some clarity." the notepad is now with me.

I wondered through her curls of silence, and it was then i wanted her to come closer to me and speak in my heart, possibly that was happening already.

She came with total clarity where her music was only breathing; it was so simple that all of the commotions around me ultimately concluded, it was her and her absolute stillness.

She was reading Shiva to Shankara, which i finished in one day to impress her that i can read for you which went un-noticed. The only thing i got from her is a smile and an expression of amazement.

Shiva to Shankara was about completing the other half of a hermit through various means of material and spiritual methods. Goddess transforms shiva in householder, a being of regenerative energy.

It was her way of transforming my energy into something creative. I wanted to do it myself, but i think there was a need for her to complete it.

We exchanged communication through a note, writing back and forth without transferring much from lips. It was not required; meanwhile, Anurag was gaping what is going on.

She asked me, "how close do you feel yourself?" , "She wanted to smile, but she was stopping it."

She also mentioned that she has some chaos, running through her life,

I wanted to know everything about her, did not wish to go beyond the idea of trying, not worth it, let things reveal itself to order of improvable.

Observing her unbeknown closely, I expected her to be around since she has to come back for her book.

She came, and we again exchanged silence, she said she has to go for her dhyana. I asked her if i can join her? She said yes, but somehow there was a force which wouldn't let me do that (Force of social prejudice, i hope she can get out of it, there is no need to define anything to anyone)

In the end, the time came where she said. I have to go Sarnath would you want to join me, after asking her that if there is a way that i can join her in silence, Sarnath and yes, i wanted to go anywhere for her.

She said let's meet at 4.30 in the morning , it was raining whole night , i was wondering how will she manage to come out , i messaged her around 3.45 that hey, its raining do you want to go, she said it's your call we can meet in the morning, i said no, lets meet now. She left with her phone number on the notepad.

The night was small, raining.

No way to communicate, no money, i was nothing there was an old guy a rickshaw puller (Tri-cycle) he said to me let me first have tea then we will leave, i said no, let's go now, you can drink there on the crossing of godowlia,

We left, i could see water everywhere it was flooded, i guess i was wondering what is going to happen but not wondering anything beyond that point, flowing.

Given that my eyes cannot see far it was all distortion in front of me,
I could not see her at the crossing. Rickshaw guy started drinking his tea and asked me to call her. I couldn't say much to him. I was looking around and asking him to wait. He was kind towards my behavior.

We were supposed to meet there but after messaging Anurag and then using my laptop to get in touch with her. I was at ease that she was inside an ATM, i had to ask her money also to pay this rickshaw guy. For my behavior, he charged 100 rupees.

Then it all started.

Rain is not going to stop now,
This place is an escape from VNS, Sleepy town
Beautiful place to be here for silence
Whither? To Sarnath, possibly around 10 KMS,
Do you want to speak
There was a snake in her finger. I am a snake. Also, i could not tell her. It was copper. I have copper also in my body.

After a 10 km in an Auto, we stopped
Let's go to the temple, Persistence of an auto driver to stay there and wait for us without taking any money.
Like he has to deliver us to those gates.
I said it would take time. The auto guy said it is ok you go.
Probably the auto guy left.

Meditation in silence in the first temple,
Tea break it was,
I want to break my silence for you, but i am not sure

Not sure where to go and what to do, some monasteries

Someone is waiting for us in one of the monasteries we did not have to try
We were love and wisdom.

I am still learning flute, her sister also play
Its an alchemy of my breathing
The pipe is closer to my heart.

IATA codes for cities VNS and LKO, i asked her what is for Pune, she did not know.

The less i know, the more i remember.

Its an iteration of actions, a loop where if the conditions break
You are quiet. Reaction over contemplation.

I am going to laugh like an idiot, and I am the right person to answer everything there are no mundane reactions,

I swear to this earth. I am compassionate. I am god, simple, basic Complexity is not intelligence; it could be you are dumb, in the order of social fabric, where everything is complex

I talk to myself. I am talking to myself not-realizing that this whole illusion is my creation. Why fear something when this is not real, fear is also not real. Death is not the end for this illusion; Anurag thinks that this whole world is a simulation a code.

I don't wish to know who i was in past life.
Near-death i was, now we are going to paradoxes.
Something personal, don't imagine anything.
I know i am going to live 80 years.

Do we change the body
Do i believe that death is not the end?
Are you aware of yourself?

You are loose,
the fear of not using time properly if surrounded by people.
I don't feel lonely
i have learned to live alone
Exclusively loved by nature.
I don't get stuck in mundane thoughts,
Slap me,

Who gets to decide who lives or dies?
Why some people die and some not, but eventually others die.
It seems like a mystery or misery.
I wonder what my story is. I am not asking your usual life story.

I am an imaginary person. The identity does not exist.
I want to exist after this world.
Gain your consciousness. You can live forever.
What about your filters, where did you lose them.

Ah, i am a pandora box.
No, i am not, i want to be nothing
Wanting to be nothing is also a want where you want the no, thing.
Zero, i am.
I have understood everything as it is.

My existing is not intentional, but i do know
this body allows me to gain consciousness
Hoping to happen.
I am sure it's infinite.

Low tides, high tides. The cycle of energy, consciousness as matter,
A room dark full of matter, the light comes, and you see, how you see that is consciousness
It's the eye,

I am ekant.

Did you talk to a tree?
I used to sit under the tree for hours and write poems.

Vipassana, i tried but couldn't go, now heading there
I want to go inside.
What are you playing
Some memories and abstract form from the future and past.

I want to leave if you're going to
Everything is on me.
Do i look weird, why people are staring at me?

I have been dynamic in Benaras,
Get rid of your hair, and i want to have that confidence one day.
Not today then never.

I walk a lot, let's hear some music, let's play
Lets dance, let go back
Some plans never work out.
Burning ghats, that's where i die.
Now i know everything about myself.

Contemplation above reaction, a passage acts as inertia.

I have been pushed to understand that silence means the absence of meaning; words can be manipulating and corruptive; silence is purity.

Learn this from the waters: in mountain clefts and chasms, loud gush the streamlets, but great rivers flow silently.

It never happened, an illusion which we probably never want to accept.

Touch and Experience

The real experience came from her touch, where i asked her and introduced to contact dance, she understood it while in motion with me. Her hands were ready and receiving my touch. I was hesitating before she was open about my indulgence in her body.

Illusion to reality, she came to me and hugged before leaving, i wanted more, i proposed to kiss her.

I walked behind her when she started running, and she knew if she would stay there with me, it is going to be one, nothing will remain because when zero divides something greater then zero it goes infinite she resisted infinity.

She left without saying much. Finally, i ran towards her and said goodbye, she replied, how do you know this is our last meeting.

I am zero, and she is nothing, indeterminant.

I am burning alive.

It was the end where we sat next to pyres of Benaras; we were burning alive, and the process was in front of us. Dissolving in fire and thus in ashes, nothing can stop this, i wanted to, but poor me i tried.

Permanence is an illusion; nothing holds in the event of death. The silence of the cosmos felt when i die, all of my resolves come to an end without suffering i am at ultimate ease.

Date Around Ending of March 2018
Location Pune

A collection of my mind within my mind (self-referencing) where i just get lost, and it comes back with all of these thoughts which i cannot reach to finality.

Logical consistency is smooth, but thoughts are diverse, they are asymmetric. How can i prove my self?

Jumping on from one thought to another is what i do? Is that impulsive No, sometimes you can refer that as fast decision making. Sometimes it is slow in some cases. That is incompleteness.

References of identification of the idea of consciousness which exist within us in some form. Like nature of reality which we are in right now.

What is consciousness? I wonder, even though i have an idea but i would still wonder because i am looking outside towards the physical reality.

Could it be a matter? Just like solid rock, just like water and so forth all these questions revolve within my patterned life of mind which i have created.

To understand the fundamental reality of nature? Do i need a universal language? For the first time, I am thinking about the essential nature of reality, although most of the times i am concerned about women, money, and sex.

For a moment i enter into this space of observer and how do i put the observer into a specific role i find it quite hard. The one who looks at the view outside for instance this is my subjective experience about the motion of a vehicle which i am sitting right now.

Why am i am experiencing this life form at all? It's hard if you are observing this. Hang on, and I have something interesting for you.[1]

Dualism comes into the picture now, and I can separate myself from this vehicle because it does not have an anima or soul.

Who is who moving who?

If the soul is moving my body which is made up of atoms?

The physical reality the laws governing our universe is pushing my body then what the purpose of this soul is? If my essence only contains the thinking thing which i have and then what my body is doing? Can the body live without the substance or vice versa?

---

[i] https://digital.usfsp.edu/fac_publications/198/
[ii] https://digital.library.lse.ac.uk/objects/lse:diz789zox

www.ingramcontent.com/pod-product-compliance
Lightning Source LLC
Chambersburg PA
CBHW030455220526
45464CB00006B/2548